No Backbone!
The World of Invertebrates

Hidden Walkingsticks

by Meish Goldish

Consultant: Brian V. Brown
Curator, Entomology Section
Natural History Museum of Los Angeles County

BEARPORT
PUBLISHING

NEW YORK, NEW YORK

Credits

Cover, © Patricio Robles Gil/SIERRA MADRE/Minden Pictures; 4–5, © Luiz Claudio Marigo/Nature Picture Library; 6, © Robert & Linda Mitchell; 7, © age fotostock/SuperStock; 8, © Joel Sartore/National Geographic/Getty Images; 9, © REUTERS/Peter Macdiarmid; 10, © Kevin Schafer/Alamy; 11, © Pascal Goetgheluck/Ardea; 12, © Ronald F. Billings, Texas Forest Service, Bugwood.org; 13, © Art Wolfe, Inc.; 14, © Jim Brandenburg/Minden Pictures; 15, © Patricio Robles Gil/ SIERRA MADRE/Minden Pictures; 17, © Piotr Naskrecki/Minden Pictures; 18, © Piotr Naskrecki/Minden Pictures; 19, © Maximilian Weinzierl/Alamy; 20, © Anthony Bannister; Gallo Images/Corbis; 21, © Patricio Robles Gil/Nature Picture Library; 22TL, © Michael Fogden/Animals Animals-Earth Scenes; 22TR, © Nicola Vernizzi/Shutterstock; 22BL, © Creatas/ SuperStock; 22BR, © Peter Wey/Shutterstock; 23TL, © age fotostock/SuperStock; 23TR, © Jim Wehtje/Photodisc Green/ Getty Images; 23BL, © Joel Sartore/National Geographic/Getty Images; 23BR, © Maximilian Weinzierl/Alamy.

Publisher: Kenn Goin
Editorial Director: Adam Siegel
Creative Director: Spencer Brinker
Design: Dawn Beard Creative
Photo Researcher: Elaine Soares

Library of Congress Cataloging-in-Publication Data

Goldish, Meish.
 Hidden walkingsticks / by Meish Goldish.
    p. cm. — (No backbone! The world of invertebrates series)
 Includes bibliographical references and index.
 ISBN-13: 978-1-59716-646-1 (library binding)
 ISBN-10: 1-59716-646-4 (library binding)
 1. Stick insects—Juvenile literature. I. Title.

 QL509.5.G65 2008
 595.7'29—dc22
                              2007038530

For more information, write to Bearport Publishing Company, Inc., 101 Fifth Avenue, Suite 6R, New York, New York 10003. Printed in the United States of America.

10 9 8 7 6 5 4 3 2 1

Contents

Animal or Plant?

Walkingsticks are brown or green **insects** that look like twigs.

They hide easily on trees and other plants.

Their color and shape help them blend in with branches and leaves.

Often, other animals cannot tell that a walkingstick is right next to them!

A Stick-Like Body

Every part of a walkingstick's body is long and thin.

The insect has six legs for walking and two **antennas** for feeling and smelling.

It also has a hard covering called an exoskeleton.

An exoskeleton protects the soft inner parts of an insect's body.

antennas

legs

wings

Most insects are good fliers, but many walkingsticks cannot fly well. Some have very small wings. Others have no wings at all.

Short and Long

There are more than 2,500 kinds of walkingsticks.

Their size depends on where they live.

In the United States, most walkingsticks are about 4 inches (10 cm) long.

In hot, rainy forests around the world, they may be 12 inches (30 cm) long.

In Asia, people found a walkingstick more than 21 inches (53 cm) long. It is the longest known insect.

Leafy Meals

Walkingsticks eat the leaves on trees and other plants.

Some spend their whole lives eating and living on one plant.

Others walk from plant to plant to find food.

Sometimes, groups of walkingsticks eat every leaf from several trees that are close together.

Like all insects that chew and eat leaves, walkingsticks have powerful jaws.

Dangerous Neighbors

Walkingsticks don't eat other animals, but some animals like to eat them.

These enemies include birds, frogs, spiders, and lizards.

Sometimes deer and other animals that eat twigs and leaves eat walkingsticks by mistake!

spider

walkingstick

frog

walkingstick

13

Hiding from Enemies

Walkingsticks hide from enemies by keeping still most of the day.

They move only to make it look like they are twigs swaying in the wind.

Other animals are usually fooled and leave them alone.

Walkingsticks walk and eat only at night, when they are hidden by darkness.

14

Fighting Back

Once in a while, a hungry animal is able to spot a walkingstick.

When this happens, some walkingsticks poke their enemies with the spikes on their legs.

Others give off a bad smell that drives away attackers.

Some spray a liquid that makes an enemy go blind for a short time.

Walkingsticks with wings may spread them to scare animals away.

17

Starting Out

Female walkingsticks lay tiny, hard eggs that look like plant seeds.

Some females bury their eggs to hide them.

Others lay them high up in a tree and let them drop to the ground.

It takes between a few months and a year for the eggs to hatch, depending on the kind of walkingstick.

The babies that come out are called **nymphs**.

eggs

nymph

egg

Walkingstick nymphs look like tiny adults when they hatch.

19

Getting Big

The bodies of walkingstick nymphs grow fast.

Their exoskeletons cannot get bigger, however.

So the nymphs molt—shedding their old coverings and forming new ones.

After six or seven molts, the nymphs have become adults.

They are "big twigs" at last!

old exoskeleton

walkingstick

Some walkingsticks grow up in three months. Other kinds take a year to become adults.

21

A World of Invertebrates

An animal that has a skeleton with a **backbone** inside its body is a *vertebrate* (VUR-tuh-brit). Mammals, birds, fish, reptiles, and amphibians are all vertebrates.

An animal that does not have a skeleton with a backbone inside its body is an *invertebrate* (in-VUR-tuh-brit). More than 95 percent of all kinds of animals on Earth are invertebrates.

Some invertebrates, such as insects and spiders, have hard skeletons—called exoskeletons—on the outside of their bodies. Other invertebrates, such as worms and jellyfish, have soft, squishy bodies with no exoskeletons to protect them.

Here are four insects that are closely related to walkingsticks. Like all insects, they are invertebrates.

Leaf Insect

Praying Mantis

Cricket

Grasshopper

Glossary

antennas
(an-TEN-uhz)
the two body parts
on a walkingstick's
head used for
feeling and
smelling

backbone
(BAK-*bohn*)
a group of
connected bones
that run along
the backs of some
animals, such as
dogs, cats, and fish;
also called a spine

insects (IN-sekts)
small animals that
have six legs, three
main body parts,
two antennas, and
a hard covering
called an exoskeleton

nymphs (NIMFS)
young insects that
change into adults
by growing and
shedding their
exoskeleton again
and again

Index

Read More

Green, Emily K. *Walkingsticks.* Minneapolis, MN: Bellwether Media (2007).

Harris, Monica. *Walking Stick.* Chicago: Heinemann Library (2003).

Howard, Fran. *Walkingsticks.* Mankato, MN: Capstone Press (2005).

Learn More Online

To learn more about walkingsticks, visit
www.bearportpublishing.com/NoBackbone-Insects

About the Author

Meish Goldish has written more than 100 books for children.
He lives in Brooklyn, New York.